W9-BMR-256

JESUS
DAY BY DAY

Jesus: Day by Day
Copyright © 2008 by Beth Moore
All Rights Reserved

ISBN 978-0-8054-4855-9
B&H Publishing Group
Nashville, Tennessee
BHPublishingGroup.com

Unless otherwise noted, all Scripture
quotations are taken from the Holman
Christian Standard Bible® copyright ©
1999, 2000, 2002, 2003 by Holman Bible
Publishers.

Printed in Singapore
1 2 3 4 5 12 11 10 09 08

JESUS
DAY BY DAY

BETH
MOORE

PUBLISHING GROUP

NASHVILLE, TENNESSEE

He is Jesus.

The One and Only.

Transcendent over all else.

To know Him is to love Him.

To love Him is to long for Him.

To long for Him is to finally reach

soul hands into the One true thing

we need never get enough of.

Jesus.

Take all you want.

Take all you need.

Till soul is fed.

And spirit freed.

Till dust is dust.

And Face you see.

Jesus Christ.

He's all you need.

You will conceive and give birth to a son,
and you will call His name JESUS.
   —Luke 1:31

Do you realize this was the first proclamation of our Savior's name since the beginning of time?

Jesus—the very name at which every knee will one day bow. The very name that every tongue will one day confess. A name that has no parallel in my vocabulary or yours. A name I whispered into the ears of my infant daughters as I rocked them and sang lullabies of His love. A name by which I've made every single prayerful petition of my life. A name that has meant my absolute salvation, not only from eternal destruction but from myself.

A name with power like no other name.

Jesus.

What a beautiful name. I love to watch how it falls off the lips of those who love Him. I shudder as it falls off the lips of those who don't.

It has been the most important and most consistent word in my life. Dearer today than yesterday. Inexpressibly precious.

Jesus.

You were washed, you were sanctified, you were justified in the name of the Lord Jesus Christ and by the Spirit of our God.
    —1 Corinthians 6:11

Mary asked the angel, "How can this be, since I have not been intimate with a man?"
—Luke 1:34

I wonder if Mary knew when He arrived in her womb. Brothers in the faith might be appalled that I would ask such a question, but female minds were created to think intimate, personal thoughts like these!

I have at least a hundred questions to ask Mary in heaven. And no doubt Mary will have some interesting stories to tell. Part of the fun of heaven will be hearing spiritual giants tell the details of the old, old stories.

Mary certainly wouldn't have thought of herself as a spiritual giant, would she?

Could a teenager have fathomed that she was to give birth to the Son who was the radiance of God's glory and the exact representation of His being?

Oh yes, the news was good. The best. But the news was also hard. When the winds of heaven converge with the winds of earth, lightning is bound to strike. Seems to me that Gabriel left just in time for Mary to tell her mother. And I have a feeling Nazareth was about to hear and experience a little thunder!

For the Father Himself loves you, because you have loved Me and have believed that I came from God.
    —John 16:27

When Elizabeth heard Mary's greeting, the
baby leaped inside her, and Elizabeth was
filled with the Holy Spirit.
   —Luke 1:41

The two women had one important
predicament in common—questionable
pregnancies, sure to stir up some talk.

Elizabeth hadn't been out of the house in
months. It makes you wonder why. As
happy as she was, it must have been
strange not to blame her sagging figure
and bumpy thighs on the baby. And to
think she was forced to borrow maternity
clothes from her friends' granddaughters.

But maybe Elizabeth and Mary were too
busy talking between themselves to pay
much attention. Can you imagine their

conversation over tea? One too old, the other too young. One married to an old priest, the other promised to a young carpenter. One heavy with child, the other with no physical evidence to fuel her faith. But God had graciously given them one another with a bond to braid their lives forever.

Women are like that, aren't they? We long to find someone who has been where we've been, who shares our fragile places, who sees our sunsets with the same shades of blue.

He comforts us in all our affliction, so that we may be able to comfort those who are in any kind of affliction, through the comfort we ourselves receive from God.
—*2 Corinthians 1:4*

From now on all generations will call me
blessed, because the Mighty One has done
great things for me, and His name is holy.
    —Luke 1:48–49

Mary had probably been too scared to
celebrate before, but Elizabeth's confirma-
tion of God's miraculous work set her
free! Whether or not young Mary began
physically jumping up and down with joy
and excitement, her insides certainly did!

I am totally blessed by the thought.
Nothing is more appropriate than getting
excited when God does something in our
lives. I think He loves it!

Scripture draws a picture here of a
reflective young woman with an unusual
heart for God. Her statement that "all

generations will call me blessed" was not voiced in pride but from shock. God seems to love little more than stunning the humble with His awesome brand of intervention.

Please don't lose the wonder of this. Marvel with me at the fact that Mary was plain, simple, and extraordinarily ordinary. I always felt the same way growing up. Still do, deep down inside.

That's part of the beauty of God choosing someone like you and me to know Him and serve Him. May we never get over it.

There is no one holy like the Lord. There is no one besides You! And there is no rock like our God.
    —1 Samuel 2:2

*In those days a decree went out from
Caesar Augustus that the whole empire
should be registered.*
    —Luke 2:1

I have heard the questions thousands of
times: Why do we celebrate Christmas on
December 25? How do we know when
the birth of Christ took place? Why
celebrate Christmas at a time originally
set aside for ancient pagan celebrations?

In the Jewish calendar, the fourteenth
day of the first month is called the day of
conception. If our God of perfect
planning and gloriously significant order
happened to overshadow Mary on the
fourteenth day of the first month of His
calendar, our Savior would have been
born toward the end of our December.

We have absolutely no way of knowing whether or not He did.

But I would not be the least bit surprised for God to have sparked His Son's human life on one Passover . . . and ended it on another.

No, I don't believe in Easter bunnies, and I don't have much of an opinion on Santa Clauses, but I am a hopeless romantic when it comes to celebrating Christmas, the birth of my Savior. Until a further "Hear ye! Hear ye!" comes from heaven, December 25 works mighty fine for me.

Go and eat what is rich, drink what is sweet, and send portions to those who have nothing prepared, since today is holy to our Lord.
— Nehemiah 8:10

*While they were there, the time came for her
to give birth.*
　—Luke 2:6

The time. The time toward which all
"time" had been ticking since the
kingdom clock struck one.

These words in Luke 2:6 refer to the most
important segment of time since the first
tick of the clock. The second hand circled
tens of thousands of times for thousands
of years, then finally, miraculously,
majestically—the time came. God's voice
broke through the barrier of the natural
realm through the cries of an infant,
startled by life on the outside.

The Son of God had come to earth,
wrapped in a tiny cloak of human flesh.

"She wrapped Him snugly in cloth and laid Him in a feeding trough—because there was no room for them at the inn" (Luke 2:7).

Father God, You have brought all things together in Christ—things both in heaven and on earth. Therefore, we who have put our hope in Jesus our Messiah praise His glorious name (Eph. 1:10, 12). Obedient to Your call, He has met us in our deepest need . . . just when we needed Him most.

But when the completion of the time came, God sent His Son, born of a woman, born under the law, to redeem those under the law.
    —Galatians 4:4–5

The angel said to them, "Don't be afraid, for look, I proclaim to you good news of great joy that will be for all the people."
    —Luke 2:10

Luke 2 identifies the first persons to receive the glorious announcement of Christ's birth. How do you think the glory of the Lord looked around the shepherds? Why do you think He first proclaimed such good news to a motley crew of sheepherders?

He just seems to enjoy revealing Himself to common people rather than to those who feel most worthy. He often uses the foolish things of this world to confound the wise. Maybe God had a soft place in His heart for the shepherds watching over their flocks.

Oh, how I love Him. The untouchable Hand of God reaching down to touch the fallen hand of man. How I thank Him that we who were once alienated and hostile toward Him because of our evil actions have been reconciled through Christ's death. Even more, we who deserved death and shame have been presented before Him holy, faultless, and blameless (Col. 1:21–22).

May we live to worship You, Lord, for such amazing grace. And may we live to tell of its wonders to others.

God has chosen the world's insignificant and despised things—the things viewed as nothing—so He might bring to nothing the things that are viewed as something.
    —1 Corinthians 1:28

But Mary was treasuring up all these things in her heart and meditating on them.
—Luke 2:19

She closed her eyes and listened, stealing time like a hidden metronome, as high and as wide as she dared to think, but she still could not begin to comprehend. She, a common child of the most humble means who had never read the Scriptures for herself, was embracing the incarnate Word. The fullness of the Godhead rested in her inexperienced arms, sleeping to the rhythm of her heart.

She hummed a song she did not know, a song being sung by the choir of angels hovering over her head but hidden from her carnal senses. The deafening hallelujahs of the heavenly hosts were silent to mortal ears except through the sounds of a young woman's voice who had unknowingly given human notes to a holy score.

The tiny baby boy had robbed her heart. "So, this is how it feels to be a mother," she mused.

She crept back into the stable, wrapped Him in swaddling clothes and laid Him in the manger. Just down the path, the sun peeked gently over the roof of an inn full of barren souls who had made Him no room.

May my meditation be pleasing to Him;
I will rejoice in the LORD.
    —Psalm 104:34

When the days of their purification according to the law of Moses were finished, they brought Him up to Jerusalem to present Him to the Lord.

—Luke 2:22

Each of the steps Mary and Joseph took after Christ's birth was typical of devout Jewish parents. What made it atypical is that their infant would ultimately fulfill the prophetic representation of each of these rituals.

When Jewish parents presented their firstborn son to the Lord, they were symbolizing the act of giving him up by saying, "He is Yours and we give him back to You." Then they would immediately redeem him or, in effect, buy him back with their offerings.

How interesting, though, that the New Testament tells us Christ came to fulfill for us the very rite Mary and Joseph observed as they presented the Christ child to the Lord.

The Word made flesh first entered the temple wrapped in a baby blanket. His earthly parents lifted Him to His Father and, in essence, purchased Him from heaven—for a while—for a lost world.

One day that baby would buy them from earth for the glory of heaven. Wow.

In Him we have redemption through His blood, the forgiveness of our trespasses, according to the riches of His grace.
    —Ephesians 1:7

*All those who heard Him were astounded at
His understanding and His answers.*
 —Luke 2:47

Left behind at the temple, seated with the
Jewish teachers, we don't know if God
allowed the twelve-year-old Christ to
exercise His full omniscience or to
unleash just enough wisdom to astound
His listeners. But we do know that not
only did He listen and ask them questions, He answered them!

There are several examples in Scripture
of Jesus posing a question that only He
could answer. He certainly uses that
method with me.

Sometimes He'll cause me to dig through
Scripture for a question He seemed to

initiate. Other times the question may come as a personalized whisper in my heart: "Beth, why are you acting that way?" Often my honest answer is, "I don't know, Lord. Can You tell me why?" If I really search His heart, He'll sooner or later give me insight into my reactions. He answers me, so that I don't have to live off my own answers.

If the boy Christ could answer difficult questions, surely we can trust the immortal One seated at the right hand of God to make intercession for us and give us new understanding.

They were astonished at His teaching because His message had authority.
    —Luke 4:32

"Why were you searching for Me?"
He asked them. "Didn't you know that
I had to be in my Father's house?"
  —Luke 2:49

Mary, understandably hurt that Jesus
had chosen to hang back in Jerusalem
and leave them to worry about His safety,
asked Him a question: "Son, why have
you treated us like this?" Christ's
response suggests He was as mystified
that they'd expect to find Him anywhere
else as they were mystified to find
Him there.

In my opinion, Christ's response was
quite interesting. I've searched every
Greek translation I can find, and none of
my resources have an original word that
directly translates to "house" or "business"

in verse 49. From what I can gather, a more precise translation of Christ's response might be: "Didn't you know that I had to be about my Father?"

That question implies the desire of my heart more than any other I can imagine. I just want to be about God. Not about ministry. Not about my own agenda. Not about writing books and Bible studies. Not about me at all. When all is said and done, I would give my life for people to be able to say, "She was just about God." That would be the ultimate legacy.

I also consider everything to be a loss in view of the surpassing value of knowing Christ Jesus my Lord.
    —Philippians 3:8

*Jesus increased in wisdom and stature, and in
favor with God and with people.*
   —Luke 2:52

People didn't just respect Jesus—they
liked Him. The word "favor" is undeni-
ably related to the word "favorite." I don't
believe we are stretching the text in the
least to say that Christ was a favorite of
many who knew Him.

Think for a few moments of the different
characteristics of people who tend to
capture your favor. Unless those characteristics are inconsistent with godliness,
in all likelihood Christ possessed them.
I can readily share a few of my favorite
characteristics in people: godly, warm
and personable, at least somewhat
demonstrative, knowledgeable in a

specific area so I can learn from them, trustworthy, and funny!

I simply want you to be reminded that He was real. His sandals flapped when He walked down the road. His hair was misshapen when He awakened. He had to brush the bread crumbs off His beard after He ate. The muscles in His arms flexed when He lifted His little brothers and sisters. He had hair on His arms and warmth in His palms.

He was the Son of God and the Son of man. Fathom the unfathomable.

The boy grew up and became strong, filled with wisdom, and God's grace was on Him.
  —Luke 2:40

They were baptized by him in the Jordan
River as they confessed their sins.
—Matthew 3:6

Picture John waist-deep in water with
people streaming out to be baptized—
baptizing them unto repentance,
preparing them to encounter the Savior.

I believe they were quite specific
confessing their sins. In all likelihood
they were crying out these confessions,
maybe even wailing, weeping over them.

Then came Christ. He was not coming to
be baptized unto repentance. He was the
spotless Lamb of God. Complete perfection. He was the only One who had no
confessing to do that day in those waters.
He came for John to baptize Him.

But I see something so precious in the fact that the people had confessed their sins standing in those same waters. He was baptized—drenched in the same waters where they had confessed their sins. Can you almost see Him wearing the sins they had confessed there?

Those of us who have already received Christ have been baptized into Him. Now daily confession and repentance is like refreshment to our souls. We come away cleansed. Ready to be filled. Ready to walk in the Spirit.

It is I who sweep away your transgressions for My own sake and remember your sins no more.
    —Isaiah 43:25

John tried to stop Him, saying, "I need to be
baptized by You, and yet You come to me?"
    —Matthew 3:14

Our gloriously deliberate God orches-
trated the lives of two extraordinary men,
born six months apart, to converge
waist-deep in the waters of the Jordan
River. For John the Baptizer, it was the
beginning of the end. He had faithfully
prepared God's way, and now God was
preparing his.

For Jesus, it marked the end of the
beginning. His life would descend on
Galilee, Judea, and Jerusalem like a desert
storm. That day in the river of promise,
John baptized Jesus with water, and Jesus
baptized the Jordan with glory.

Just imagine what was going on in the mind of Christ as He was walking to the river Jordan. I wonder if He stopped to watch the scene for a while, with the people confessing their sins. Did He watch this mighty servant of God preaching the Word with boldness? I'm just picturing the horizon and His figure overlooking the scene. He walks up to the shore, and John sees Him.

John had prepared for this all his life. When we set apart our lives unto Him, He will do wonders with us the likes of which we cannot imagine.

When I saw Him, I fell at His feet like a dead man. He laid His right hand on me, and said, "Don't be afraid!"
    —*Revelation 1:17*

There came a voice from heaven: "This is My beloved Son. I take delight in Him!"
   —Matthew 3:17

I believe part of God's purpose for sending Jesus here was to experience life as we do. That means I don't believe He had X-ray vision every single second into the throne room of God. So what a time this must have been to capture that moment when He could see heaven open and the Holy Spirit descend.

And then to hear His Father's blessing.

Again, I don't think God spoke audibly to His Son every day He was on earth. I think maybe Jesus was called here to sympathize with us and to take part in the same kind of relationship we do.

A whole lot of His prayer was spent talking to God, knowing only in His own spirit and through God's Word what the Father was answering Him. Like us.

So the audible voice of His Father sounding forth at His baptism must have just fallen on Jesus with the dearest of familiarity. I want to think that through the night, He replayed that voice and blessing in His own mind a thousand times. "He loves Me. Life is hard here, but He's proud of Me. I have the blessing. I have the blessing!"

He is the image of the invisible God,
the firstborn over all creation.
    —Colossians 1:15

Jesus returned from the Jordan, full of the
Holy Spirit, and was led by the Spirit in
the wilderness for 40 days to be tempted
by the Devil.
    —Luke 4:1–2

God's Word tells us that Christ was
tempted just as we are. So I believe that
long before He was thirty years old,
Christ experienced numerous other
temptations exactly like those we face in
our day-to-day struggles. What thirty-
year-old hasn't been tempted?

Yet although Christ's experience in the
desert wasn't His first grapple with
temptation, it did represent an intense
season that was tailored by the enemy for
the challenges of messiahship that lay
ahead. Some issues were meant to be

settled from the very beginning of Christ's ministry.

Satan is very shrewd. He probably won't tempt you to turn stones into bread, assume authority over the kingdoms of the world, or throw yourself off the highest point of the temple. He designs temptations to each person's challenges. But we can learn from Christ's response to these extraordinary tests. Scripture is always the most powerful tool in our fight against temptation. Don't fight back with *your* words. Fight back with God's!

We do not have a high priest who is unable to sympathize with our weaknesses, but One who has been tested in every way as we are, yet without sin.
   —Hebrews 4:15

The Spirit of the Lord is on Me, because He has anointed Me to preach good news to the poor.
—Luke 4:18

I was a mess before the Savior set me free. That's why my dearest life passages are the ones found in Isaiah 61:1–2 and quoted again in the Gospel of Luke. Jesus went to His home synagogue in Nazareth and declared the nature of His call and ministry—to preach good news to the poor, to heal the brokenhearted, to proclaim freedom for the prisoners, sight for the blind, to release the oppressed, and to proclaim the year of the Lord's favor (Luke 4:18–19).

Do you know this Jesus? Once you do, you can't get over Him. Abundant life was not mine until I let the Healer set me free, not just from hell itself but from myself.

If you compare Luke 4:18–19 with the original job description of the Messiah in Isaiah 61, you will notice that Jesus abruptly stopped reading without saying "and the day of vengeance of our God." When Christ returns, He will come for His own, but He will also come with a vengeance. In His first advent, however, God purposely sent Christ with a different agenda.

Their compassionate One will guide them,
and lead them to springs of water.
    —Isaiah 49:10

They were all speaking well of Him and were amazed by the gracious words that came from His mouth, yet they said, "Isn't this Joseph's son?"
    —Luke 4:22

The crowd's mood went from admiration to a murderous rage in the moments of Christ's confrontation. Luke describes them as furious, enraged. The north wind of their admiration had suddenly reversed into a south wind of tornadic proportions. When a mood can change in a matter of moments from admiration to murderous fury, something is amiss.

The types of crowds Christ encountered two thousand years ago still fill many churches today. Many congregations want to hear impressive A+ messages, but the messenger better keep his confrontational thoughts to himself. The same committee that throws out the red carpet to a new preacher may eventually roll him out the door in it! Meanness at church sometimes exceeds anything that occurs in secular surroundings.

I believe Christ's experience in Nazareth was a pivotal moment in His life. He had to choose to perform ministry either their way or His way.

Let us then go to Him outside the camp, bearing His disgrace. For here we do not have an enduring city; instead, we seek the one to come.
    —Hebrews 13:13–14

*Leave us alone! What do You have to do
with us, Jesus—Nazarene? Have You come to
destroy us? I know who You are—the Holy
One of God!*
—Luke 4:34

Christ's earthly ministry had hardly
been launched before the demonic world
confronted Him—in a synagogue, no
less. Thank goodness, Christ isn't spooked
by the demonic world.

The demon seemed to be telling some
semblance of the truth, but we see a
distortion or misuse of the truth in the
demonic testimony. He was acting as a
counterfeit preacher of sorts. Since he
could not stop the truth, he hoped to
disqualify the message by the instability
or insanity of the apparent messenger.

Some years ago, a man who appeared to be mentally ill would stand outside the main doors of our church and "preach" to us using a megaphone as we left the building after worship. Some of his statements were technically scriptural, but the typical listener's tendency would be to disbelieve anything he said simply because he was the one saying it.

Noise and distraction. These remain the enemy's stock-in-trade. But no matter what authority Satan has been temporarily allowed in this world system, Christ can pull rank any time He wants.

A sound of uproar from the city! A voice from the temple—the voice of the Lord, paying back His enemies what they deserve!
—Isaiah 66:6

He stood over her and rebuked the fever, and it left her. She got up immediately and began to serve them.

—Luke 4:39

When Jesus went to help Simon's mother-in-law, He "stood" or "bent over her." I don't think I'm reading too much into the picture to imagine a close encounter suggesting deep concern.

I always reacted in a similar way any time one of my children was sick. I didn't remain upright and stoic, checking off a list of symptoms. I bent over them and drew close. I'd learned from my mother that I could better gauge a temperature with my cheek on their foreheads than with a thermometer. I just could not keep my distance from a sick child.

Christ could have healed Simon's
mother-in-law from the front porch. He
didn't. He came to her and drew down
close. After all, she was in no position to
seek help for herself. He involved
Himself one-on-one with those He
helped.

Our homes today are threatened by
fevers of all sorts—ones that go far
beyond the physiological: unresolved
conflict, unforgiveness, unfaithfulness,
compromising media communications,
pornography, and more. We need Jesus
in our homes. Up close.

*Who is like the LORD our God—the One
enthroned on high, who stoops down to look
on the heavens and the earth?*
    —Psalm 113:5–6

41

Very early in the morning, while it was still
dark, He got up, went out, and made His way
to a deserted place. And He was praying there.
   —Mark 1:35

I wish I had words to express the feelings
such scriptural moments stir in me. The
thought of Christ ducking out the door
while it was still dark to find a place to be
by Himself with God floods my soul with
emotion.

I love every glimpse of the unique
relationship Father and Son shared while
Christ was on earth and His Father was in
heaven. I always wonder what Christ said
to His Father and what He saw in those
intimate moments. Did God the Father
speak audibly to Him? Or did He speak
in His heart like He does to you and me

through His Word? I can't wait to find out someday in glory.

We have no idea how often Jesus got to steal away with His Father. But I'm convinced we don't give enough thought to how challenging Christ's prison of flesh must have been to Him—the pull to be in many places at once and the challenge to prioritize not just the good but the goal: proclaiming the good news of the kingdom of God.

Seek the Lord *while He may be found; call to Him while He is near.*
—Isaiah 55:6

Jesus was going all over Galilee, teaching in their synagogues, preaching the good news of the kingdom, and healing every disease and sickness among the people.
    —Matthew 4:23

One of the biggest temptations even mature believers face is being sidetracked by the urgent. Many situations need our attention. They tempt us to let them steal our focus. Christ may have faced the same temptation when the people came to Him and tried to "keep Him from leaving them" (Luke 4:42). But preaching the good news of the kingdom of God was Christ's absolute priority.

The people's attempts to hold onto Christ may not have been limited to just the vocal and emotional. They may have hung onto Him physically too. How His heart must have broken for them. Yet He knew the best thing He could do for them was to stay true to His mission.

Can you imagine how Jesus longed for the time when His work would be accomplished and He could dwell within the hearts of all who would receive Him, never to leave them? Until then, He had a job to do. Christ ignored neither the urgent need nor the ultimate goal—but He never allowed the former to hinder the latter.

Pay careful attention, then, to how you walk—not as unwise people but as wise—making the most of the time.
    —Ephesians 5:15–16

When He had finished speaking, He said to Simon, "Put out into deep water and let down your nets for a catch."
—Luke 5:4

Jesus told Peter how to fish. Now, had Peter not already known Christ, he might have thought: "Me fisherman, You carpenter. I won't tell You how to build, and You don't tell me how to fish."

But one of the most critical reasons believers experience defeat is because we categorize only a few areas of our lives as Christ's arena. So, as if to save Him the extra trouble of dealing with things that don't concern Him, we leave Christ at church to deal with areas related to His expertise.

Satan, however, is greatly defeated when we start living the truth that every area is Christ's specialty. Whether you're a homemaker, steelworker, or CEO, Christ knows every detail associated with your job. He knows accounting, movie-theater managing, banking, drafting, engineering, nursing, real-estate brokering, and anything else we could do. For crying out loud, the One who knows the numbers of hairs on your head could also style them if He wanted! Not one of us does anything for a living that Jesus can't do better.

Now may the God of peace . . . equip you with all that is good to do His will, working in us what is pleasing in His sight.
    —Hebrews 13:20–21

He saw Jesus, fell facedown, and begged Him: "Lord, if You are willing, You can make me clean."
—Luke 5:12

Try as I might, I cannot imagine what purpose some illnesses and premature deaths serve. But after years of loving and seeking my God, I trust who He is even when I have no idea what He's doing. Above all things, I believe God always has purpose in every decision He makes. Jesus healed people many times, but His healings were always with purpose and intent.

How much like the leper are you? Are you convinced (first of all) that Christ can do absolutely anything? And secondly, are you also seeking His purposes in everything? Are you more desirous of His work and will being done through your life than you are to be healed of your hardship or handicap?

If so, don't lose courage. As long as this remains the desire of your heart, come to Christ as the leper did—humbly making your request while seeking His purposes for your life. I believe with all my heart that the central issue involved in whether or not God heals a believing and requesting Christian's physical illness is found in His eternal purpose.

LORD, *hear my voice when I call; be gracious to me and answer me. In Your behalf my heart says, "Seek My face." LORD, I will seek Your face.*
    —Psalm 27:7–8

"So you may know that the Son of Man has authority on earth to forgive sins"—He told the paralyzed man, *"I tell you: get up, pick up your stretcher, and go home."*
 —Luke 5:24

Jesus came as the Son of Man to rescue us from the great plight of man: we have a sin problem, and we are powerless to help ourselves. Given the right set of circumstances and the wrong state of mind, each of us is capable of just about anything. Even if we could get our external lives under perfect and legalistic control, we'd probably rot on the inside with the heinous sin of pride.

Let's face it, we're all hopeless—except that Jesus came as the "Son of Man" with the "authority on earth to forgive sins."

So if you have truly repented—which means you have experienced godly sorrow and a subsequent detour from sin—bathe yourself in the river of God's forgiveness. The Son of Man has authority to forgive sins right here on earth. You don't have to wait until heaven. You can experience the freedom of complete forgiveness right here. Right now.

Fall under Christ's authority and accept His grace.

He redeemed my soul from going down to the Pit, and I will continue to see the light.
    —Job 33:28

The scribes and Pharisees were watching Him
closely, to see if He would heal on the Sabbath,
so that they could find a charge against Him.
 —Luke 6:7

When the man with the shriveled hand
stood before Him on the Sabbath, Jesus
knew the Pharisees and teachers of the
law were looking to accuse Him. But He
did not allow Himself to be controlled by
potential accusations.

His public question to His accusers made
them look terribly foolish. Picture the
scene as Jesus looked around at them all.
Eye to eye. Just waiting for someone to
give Him an answer.

Then He said to the man, "Stretch out
your hand." And he did. Right there in

front of all those perfect, pious-looking people. The man who all his life had probably hidden his handicap under the sleeve of his garment stretched forth his humiliating infirmity—and was healed. It was enough to make those who were sitting by to be "filled with rage," off to their own little corners to discuss "what they might do to Jesus" (v. 11).

It's a question we must answer every time we hear or read a message from His Word. What will we do with Jesus? Will we sit under His teaching? Or just sit by?

Trust in Him at all times, you people; pour out your hearts before Him. God is our refuge.
  —Psalm 62:8

*Turning to the crowd following Him, He said,
"I tell you, I have not found so great a faith
even in Israel!"*
   —Luke 7:9

Our difficulty imagining that God could
have respect for a mere mortal like this is
because we confuse attitudes of respect
with feelings of inferiority.

We tend to view respect as a feeling we
have for those we perceive as being
superior to us. And on our best day, we
are so inferior to Christ that, if not for the
Lord's great love, we would be consumed
by holy fire.

But He created us. And He loves us. At
times, He actually delights in us. He
purposely created us with free will and

affections so that we could choose Him and love Him in the midst of many options and much opposition.

God didn't create robots. He created humans. So when God sees humans cooperate with His good work, fulfilling what they were created to be, He sees something very good. Perfect? No. But respectable? Yes. When the Father sees a human who is prone to selfishness, pride, and arrogance humble himself or herself and tremble at His Word, He esteems that person. Hallelujah! Oh, how I want to be someone God could respect!

I will look favorably on this kind of person: one who is humble, submissive in spirit, and who trembles at My word.
    —Isaiah 66:2

*When the Lord saw her, He had compassion
on her and said, "Don't cry."*
  —*Luke 7:13*

Imagine the thoughts this funeral
procession in Nain must have provoked
in the mind of the author of life.

I think the very lordship of Christ
overwhelmed Him at that moment. No
one else in the crowd could do anything
about the widow's plight. They possessed
no power. Christ was the only one
present who had lordship over the living
and the dead. His heart went out to her.
He felt deeply. He spoke only two words
to her: "Don't cry."

We've all said those two words to
someone who was brokenhearted, but I

believe Christ probably meant something a little different. I don't know about you, but most of the time when I've said to someone, "Don't cry," my heart was saying, "I can't bear to see you in so much pain!" These words usually come from one who can't stand to see the hurt because she is powerless to help.

Christ, on the other hand, is never helpless. When He said, "Don't cry," He meant, "Not only do I hurt for you, but I'm also going to do something about the cause of your hurt."

The sun of righteousness will rise with healing in its wings, and you will go out and playfully jump like calves from the stall.
—Malachi 4:2

*[John] sent a message by his disciples and
asked Him, "Are You the One who is to come,
or should we expect someone else?"*
    —Matthew 11:2–3

Like John, have you ever found yourself
waiting and waiting on Christ to come
through? Have you ever endured long
stretches of suffering on a certain matter
while hearing all sorts of wondrous
works He was doing elsewhere?

It hurts, doesn't it? We can be believers in
Jesus for years, literally seeking Him,
finding Him, and serving Him—then
suddenly have a staggering bout with
doubt. Overwhelmed with guilt and fear,
we'll think, "How in the world could I
be doubting after all this time?" It's a
horrible feeling!

I'd like to suggest, however, that these kinds of doubts are probably not coming from our heads. They're coming from our hearts. Our feelings. Our emotions. Our hurts. Does that mean we can just surrender to them? I don't think so. Our heart-doubts can be very dangerous if we remain in them. But if we wrestle through them with the Lord Jesus, when we get to the other side of our crisis, we will find ourselves spilled into a place of spacious faith!

Have mercy on some who doubt; save others by snatching them from the fire.
    —Jude 22–23

Anyone who is not offended because of Me is blessed.
  —Luke 7:23

I don't think Luke 7:23 is talking about falling away from Christ. It's talking about falling over a stumbling block into a trap.

One of Satan's most effective devices for causing a devout believer to stumble is to trap him over a matter of faith. Satan even tries to use Christ Himself against us. The most effective faith-trap Satan could set for a Christian is to tempt him or her to doubt the goodness, rightness, or mightiness of Christ.

Christ held John the Baptist in highest esteem, even after John questioned the

Lord about His messiahship. John was
under a terrible strain. His martyrdom
was imminent. Christ knew that! He
could handle John's questions because He
knew the heart and mind from which
they came.

But Jesus wanted him (and us) to be
sure we understand this: the hand of
God is at work directing divine purpose
and blessing in all the affairs of those
who don't let the perceived activity or
inactivity of Christ trap them or make
them stumble.

*For it has been given to you on Christ's behalf
not only to believe in Him, but also to suffer
for Him.*
    —Philippians 1:29

One of the Pharisees invited Him to eat with him. He entered the Pharisee's house and reclined at the table.

— Luke 7:36

Do you have difficulty picturing Christ in this scene? Do you imagine Him never fitting into a Pharisee's home? I think God desires to broaden our understanding and fine-tune some of our mental footage of Christ. The more I study His earthly life, the more I see that He could fit in anywhere . . . and nowhere.

Remember, Christ is void of all prejudice. He was no more likely to stereotype all Pharisees than He was to stereotype all who were poor, blind, or ill. Furthermore, He was just as anxious to save them from their sins. The obvious difference was how anxious the individual was to be saved.

Interestingly, not once in the Gospels do we see a Pharisee who is being confronted in the stronghold of legalism and self-righteousness ever admit to seeing it in himself. But that doesn't mean Jesus would automatically thumb his nose at an invitation just because of what this man stood for. Jesus is willing to reach into anyone's life, no matter how sinful they are or how sinless they think themselves to be.

If you show favoritism, you commit sin and are convicted by the law as transgressors.
    —James 2:9

This man, if He were a prophet, would know
who and what kind of woman this is who is
touching Him—she's a sinner!
  —Luke 7:39

Christ never downplays or minimizes sin.
Human sympathy makes excuses like,
"What you did wasn't that bad" or "After
all you've been through, no wonder . . ."

But Christ never calls sin less than it is.

So to picture Christ minimizing this
woman's sinful past is to miss the entire
point of the encounter. The point is that
even though her sins had been many,
heinous, and habitual, she had been
forgiven, saved, and liberated to love
lavishly. Of all the commandments the
Pharisee had kept, she (rather than he)

had observed the most important one: "Love the Lord your God with all your heart, with all your soul, with all your mind, and with all your strength" (Mark 12:30).

The exquisite beauty of loving Christ is that it makes it impossible to keep only one commandment. The Word tells us that the person who truly loves God will pursue the obedient life and be far more likely to persevere in trials. Loving God is the vital lifeline to all the other commandments.

I want you to be wise about what is good, yet innocent about what is evil.
    —Romans 16:19

*I tell you, her many sins have been forgiven;
that's why she loved much. But the one who is
forgiven little, loves little.*
—Luke 7:47

Customarily when I speak, someone from
the host church delivers a devotional to
the team before the conference begins.
One day a woman who did not know me,
had never heard me speak, and had never
read a single word I'd written, walked in
the door and pulled up a chair in front of
me. The entire group could hear her, but
the devotional she delivered was for me.

With obvious anointing, she told the
story of the sinful woman in the Luke 7
passage, then she said, "I don't know you,
Beth. I have no idea why God sent me
with such a message to give you, but He

told me clearly to say these words to you:
'Tell her that her many sins have been
forgiven—for she loved much.'"

Oh, how I would love to be for you today
what that woman was to me during that
difficult time. Allow me to pull up my
chair right in front of you, look you in the
eye, and tell you what He told me to say:
"Your many sins have been forgiven—
for you love much." Go in peace.

*He said to the woman, "Your faith has saved
you. Go in peace."*
    —Luke 7:50

As a large crowd was gathering, and
people were flocking to Him from every town,
He said in a parable: "A sower went out to
sow his seed."
  —Luke 8:4–5

The parable of the sower helps us
understand the obstacles that limit us
and the elements that would free the
Spirit to teach us the deep things of God.
All four types of soil represent people
who heard the Word, yet only one
produced a harvest.

It is not enough just to hear the Word!
We have stumbled on my greatest burden
for the body of Christ. How many people
sit in church services where Scripture is
never taught? They're not even hearing
the Word of God! Furthermore, what

masses of believers hear the Word but continue to live in defeat because they don't apply it?

I was one of them. I desperately wanted to change. I was miserable in my captivity. I just didn't understand that the power to be transformed was in the authentic application of Scripture. Our obedience is not to make God feel like the boss. Trust me. He's the boss and He knows it. Our obedience to apply the Word of God is so we can live victorious lives that glorify our Father in heaven. Hearing it is simply not enough.

Who has stood in the council of the LORD to see and hear His word? Who has paid attention to His word and obeyed?
　—Jeremiah 23:18

He replied to them, "My mother and My brothers are those who hear and do the word of God."
—Luke 8:21

When His mother and brothers came to see Him but could not get to Him because of the crowd, Jesus had some strong words for them. But Jesus was not rejecting His family as much as He was redefining it. His statement reflected inclusion more than exclusion.

We know, of course, that Mary certainly believed Jesus was the Son of God, but the pressure of family members can be quite forceful. Perhaps her other sons were intent on confronting Jesus, and she came along to act as a peacemaker. Sound familiar, moms? You don't have to be a

mother to imagine how she felt in her
present position.

But Christ's revolutionary words that
redefined His family dynamics are as
critical for us today as they were for those
who heard them then. According to
Luke 8:21, our kinship to Jesus Christ is
directly revealed through what we do
with the Word of God. Studying His
Word is not just a good idea. It is the
very warmth and vitality of the family
bloodline—proof that we are family
to Jesus Christ.

*The one who looks intently into the perfect
law of freedom and perseveres in it . . . will be
blessed in what he does.*
    —James 1:25

They came to Jesus and found the man the demons had departed from, sitting at Jesus' feet, dressed and in his right mind. And they were afraid.
  —Luke 8:35

The villagers came out of the woodwork only to find the talk of the region—a demon-possessed man who had the power to break ropes and chains—sitting at Jesus' feet, dressed and in his right mind. But the people allowed fear to eclipse the life-changing facts, and they begged Jesus to leave.

He could have healed them, saved them, taught them, sanctified them, and, for heaven's sake, delighted them. But all they wanted Him to do was to leave them. To go away.

So Jesus left the Gerasenes, all right. But not without a vivid reminder of who He was and what He could do. There would still be a man about town with a restored mind and real dignity who couldn't seem to hush.

How long do you think it had been since this man had been home? Not back to the tombs, but home. Clothes on his back. Roof over his head. Soundness in his mind. A message on his tongue. All the demons in the air couldn't stop him, for his knees had bowed to a new authority.

The Devil has come down to you with great fury, because he knows he has a short time.
—Revelation 12:12

He fell down at Jesus' feet and pleaded with Him to come to his house, because he had an only daughter about 12 years old, and she was at death's door.

—Luke 8:41–42

Jairus was a ruler of the synagogue, but this day no ritual dignity stood in his way. His daughter lay dying, and he threw himself at the feet of Jesus pleading for her life.

If you were to ask any set of parents how much they focus on their child when he or she is sick or in some kind of serious danger or distress, they'll tell you they can hardly focus on anything else. This was certainly the case with Jairus. Jesus was his last hope, and he was desperate for Him.

Who else could heal his little girl from the throes of death?

Whom do you know that is possibly down to his or her very last hope? Perhaps, like me, you even know several. Think of these people and keep them in your peripheral vision all day today. He is there for the desperate. He specializes in the hopeless.

Every time you think of those who are suffering, think of Jesus, who knows the path through dire need.

I am afflicted and needy; hurry to me, God. You are my help and my deliverer; Lord, do not delay.
   —Psalm 70:5

*In the presence of all the people, she declared
the reason she had touched Him and how she
was instantly cured.*
    —Luke 8:47

Jesus was on His way to heal the dying
child of Jairus when a woman in the
crowd touched the edge of His cloak.
Christ released enough power to heal her
of a twelve-year hemorrhage, but still had
plenty to raise Jairus's daughter from the
dead.

Let that sink in! Christ's power supply is
limitless! He's not the Wizard of Oz with
a limited number of wishes to grant. His
power and mercy are infinite.

Yes, He can take you much farther than
Kansas, Dorothy.

Does He seem to be on His way to another need, one that you perceive may be more important than yours? More a matter of life and death? No problem! Reach out and grab that hem! You are not going unnoticed—not even if He's on His way to raise the dead! Jesus has more than enough power!

Oh, friend, would you dare to believe that He is completely able? Will we laugh at the thought, like the foolish mourners outside Jairus's home did? Or will we be invited into the house to behold a miracle?

Indeed our fellowship is with the Father and with His Son Jesus Christ. We are writing these things so that our joy may be complete.
    —1 John 1:3–4

*Summoning the Twelve, He gave them power
and authority over all the demons, and power
to heal diseases. Then He sent them.*
—Luke 9:1–2

Up until now, the Twelve had watched
Christ at work and had witnessed His
miracles, but they had not yet been
empowered to exercise those wonders. I
don't imagine the disciples expected to do
anything but watch. But they were about
to receive a very special welcome to the
wild world of Jesus Christ.

Wouldn't you love to eavesdrop on the
conversations between the disciples as
they prepared to go out? Like us, I'm not
sure the disciples had a clue what they
had been given. They had the privilege to
be the closest earthly companions to the

Son of God. They were chosen to witness the most remarkable phenomenon in all human history: the Word made flesh and dwelling among us.

They knew the sound of His breathing when He slept. They knew His favorite foods. They watched Him heal the sick, deliver the demon-possessed, and raise the dead. If they had never received another thing, they had been granted a privilege beyond all others. But Christ didn't stop there. He also gave them power and authority.

We have not received the spirit of the world, but the Spirit who is from God, in order to know what has been freely given to us by God.
      —1 Corinthians 2:12

They went out and traveled from village to village, proclaiming the good news and healing everywhere.
—Luke 9:6

I find it interesting that Christ's instruction to His disciples to go and minister was for a specific mission or task. I believe the concepts of "calling" and "task" are often confused in the body of Christ. I know that I confused the concepts in the early years of my surrender to ministry.

The Twelve were called to be Christ's learners or pupils. They also were designated apostles, meaning they would be sent forth. But what would His pupils be sent forth to do?

Whatever He told them.

In our human need for the security of sameness, we tend to want one job assignment from God that we can do for the rest of our lives. But He's far more creative than that! You may ask, "Isn't it possible for God to assign a lifelong task such as preaching at one church for forty years?" Absolutely! But we are wise not to make assumptions by surrendering to the assignment! Our calling is to surrender to God. Think of the pitfalls we could avoid if we were more abandoned to God than to a particular kind of service.

Dear friends, we are God's children now, and what we will be has not yet been revealed.
—1 John 3:2

When Jesus looked up and noticed a huge crowd coming toward Him, He asked Philip, "Where will we buy bread so these people can eat?"

—John 6:5

Christ sometimes provokes a question so that He can be the answer. John 6:6 tells us that Christ prompted the above question to Philip "only to test him." I think Christ might have been testing His disciples to surface what they had learned or, like me, what they had yet to learn!

Think of the miracles they had seen Christ perform by this time. Yet they couldn't imagine how they were going to feed all these hungry people. I think Jesus may have been testing them to see if they were beginning to think in a "faith mode."

Their response, however, proved they still
practiced fragmented faith. While they
had seen Christ cast out demons and heal
the sick, it had not yet occurred to them
He could feed the masses.

They still had much to learn about
Christ's complete jurisdiction—that
He can meet our spiritual needs, our
emotional needs, and our physical needs.
He is both deeply spiritual and entirely
practical. Christ was teaching them to see
Him, His power, and His authority in
every area of life.

*My God will supply all your needs according
to His riches in glory in Christ Jesus.*
    —Philippians 4:19

I also say to you that you are Peter, and on this rock I will build My church, and the forces of Hades will not overpower it.
   —Matthew 16:18

When Jesus referred to the rock upon which He would build His church, I believe Christ was talking about the unchangeable, immovable testimony of Jesus Christ that Peter delivered—"You are the Messiah, the Son of the living God" (Matt. 16:16).

Jesus was saying, "Peter, the testimony of My identity is the immovable rock upon which I will build My church, the cliff on which all eternity hangs. And you are a chip off this immovable rock whom I will greatly empower." Peter was a stone that Christ would throw from place to place to give testimony to the Rock from which he was hewn.

The thought often occurs to me that Satan can do nothing to overcome the church from the outside. No amount of perversity, depravity, or even persecution will ever overcome the church. Satan can't tear us down from the outside; that's why he seeks to do an inside job using division, bitterness among believers, infighting, and denominational elitism. Local church bodies don't die because of the world's influence; they die from internal diseases. Let's be on the lookout for inside jobs.

Look to the rock from which you were cut, and to the quarry from which you were dug.
   —Isaiah 51:1

He turned and told Peter, "Get behind Me,
Satan! You are an offense to Me because you're
not thinking about God's concerns, but man's."
   —Matthew 16:23

All Satan needs to have momentary
victory over a disciple is for us to have in
mind the things of men. Satan doesn't
have to get us thinking blatantly satanic
thoughts to have victory over us. All he
needs is to get us looking at life from
man's perspective rather than God's.
But if we surrender our minds to the
things of God, we are safe! We don't have
to constantly look out for our own best
interests, because He's constantly looking
out for them.

What Peter didn't understand is that what
may have seemed best in the short run

would have been disastrous in the long run. Had Jesus saved His disciples the anxiety of His betrayal, trials, and death, He wouldn't have saved them at all.

On this earth, I don't know that we will ever perpetually have in mind the things of God rather than the things of man. But if we don't make the deliberate choice to have in mind the things of God when faced with our biggest challenges, most of us will probably default back to our natural instinct—the things of man.

As heaven is higher than earth, so My ways are higher than your ways, and My thoughts than your thoughts.
    —Isaiah 55:9

He said to them all, "If anyone wants to come with Me, he must deny himself, take up his cross daily, and follow Me."
—Luke 9:23

Those who accept this invitation are called to deny themselves. I don't believe Christ was talking about the things we typically consider self-denial. The issue here wasn't fasting from food, nor was it denying ourselves a specific extra. It wasn't about self-loathing either, because Christ clearly commanded us to love our neighbor as ourselves. I believe the primary issue involved in this kind of self-denial is denying our right to be our own authority.

I've learned the hard way that denying my right to be my own boss is what keeps me from getting slaughtered by Satan in warfare. Let's face it: this "be-your-own-boss" stuff is nothing but a myth.

But the second concept is just as vital: the recommitment to take up the cross daily. In my opinion, Dr. Luke wrote the prescription for the victorious life when He captured these words of Christ, and he wrote it for all of us who would desire to become His disciple: live life one surrendered day at a time. Eyes to the East. Hands to the cross. Feet to the path.

Who can separate us from the love of Christ? Can affliction or anguish or persecution or famine or nakedness or danger or sword?
—Romans 8:35

*Peter and those with him were in a deep sleep,
and when they became fully awake, they saw
His glory.*
   —Luke 9:32

We grow comfortable with the Christ we
know. Then suddenly He shatters the box
we've put Him in, leaving us asking,
"Who is this man?" At those times—if
we're willing—Christ will show us a
glimpse of His glory, and we will be
changed as He transfigures Himself
before us.

Jesus regularly seeks to readjust our
vision of Him. And I believe the more we
are willing to receive from Him, the more
He is willing to reveal to us. I think the
reason Jesus took Peter, James, and John
to the mountain was because they were

willing to receive greater revelation. How
blessed we truly are when we have eyes
that are willing to see and ears that are
willing to hear.

We are a direct by-product of who we
believe and who we see Christ to be.
I believe He blesses the prayer, "Father,
daily show me the reality, the greater
reality of Your Son Jesus Christ. Transfig-
ure Him before my very eyes, and then
give me the courage to adjust my life to
what I see."

*My soul, praise the LORD! LORD my God, You
are very great; You are clothed with majesty
and splendor.*
    —Psalm 104:1

*I want their hearts to be encouraged and
joined together in love, so that they may have
all the riches of assured understanding, and
have the knowledge of God's mystery—Christ.*
  —Colossians 2:2

You know what thrills me about my
husband? Even after all these years, I am
still discovering things about him. I have
security in my man—yes—but if I had
security and no mystery, that wouldn't be
any fun, would it? And if all I had was
mystery, where would the security be?
But in my husband, I have both security
and mystery.

That's what the Word of God is telling us
we all have in Christ. Don't you just love
how Jesus meets our emotional and
mental needs? He said, "You have

knowledge of Me with security, with full assurance, in relationship with who I am. But you also have constant mystery as I give You these little fragments of knowledge one at a time to open your eyes to My greatness."

Jesus has taught us so much about Himself. There is so much we can be absolutely sure of. But we will never learn it all while we're here. No matter how often we seek Him, we will always be stunned by His greatness.

On the contrary, we speak God's hidden wisdom in a mystery, which God predestined before the ages for our glory.
  —1 Corinthians 2:7

*They brought to Him a deaf man who also
had a speech difficulty, and begged Jesus to lay
His hand on him. So He took him away from
the crowd privately.*
   —Mark 7:32–33

Sometimes when Jesus is about to do
something really special in our lives, He
will rearrange our surroundings. He will
take us out of our element, just as He
took this deaf man "away from the crowd"
to give him a new perspective on God's
glory and power.

I remember how disappointed I was
when I figured out that my spiritual gift
wasn't shopping at the mall. After
becoming a serious believer and trying to
recognize what my gifts were, I discov-
ered that "fashion" wasn't even on the list

of biblical attributes. My theory was blown.

Instead, the Lord was calling me out of my element, growing in me the spiritual gift of love for the body of Christ. But to do that, He needed me in a new set of surroundings, out where He could show me that even if we speak with the tongues of angels, if we don't have love, we may as well be clanging brass. Until He has us out of our element and into His, we will never see His glory. We will always be deaf to what He's trying to say.

If I live at the eastern horizon or settle at the western limits, even there Your hand will lead me.
   —*Psalm 139:9–10*

*I brought my son to You. He has a spirit that
makes him unable to speak. . . . I asked Your
disciples to drive it out, but they couldn't.*
  —Mark 9:17–18

The teachers of the law must have been
terribly intimidating to Christ's disciples,
who were comparatively uneducated
men. We aren't always surrounded by
faith-encouragers. But we can't afford to
wait for all the atmospheric conditions
to be right before we act on the power
of God.

In fact, I think God is teaching us that
the worst conditions can often provide
the best atmosphere to act in faith. He
doesn't want our confidence regulated by
our audience. If faith-discouragers can
shake our confidence badly enough to

disable us, our confidence may be in ourselves instead of God.

I remember a time when a critical letter from a seminary graduate shook my confidence. Reading the list of mistakes she was pointing out, I started thinking, "She's right! I have no formal theological education. I shouldn't even be doing this!" But God reminded me during the following days that I was exactly right: I *shouldn't* be doing this. This ministry is God's. If my confidence is in myself, I'm in big trouble. Only One can be taken at His every word. Jesus.

We also are weak in Him, yet toward you we will live with Him by God's power.
    —2 Corinthians 13:4

Jesus said to him, "'If You can?' Everything is possible to the one who believes." Immediately the father of the boy cried out, "I do believe! Help my unbelief."
   —Mark 9:23–24

The wonderful part of the father's exclamation is his realization that, although he lacked faith, he wanted to believe! Then he did exactly what he should have done: he asked for help to overcome his unbelief.

I can't count the times I've imitated this father's actions. In my earlier days with God, I viewed faith as my willingness to make a believing statement with my mouth rather than face the questions of my heart. If only I had understood how Romans 10:10 reverses that order: "With the heart one believes, resulting in righteousness, and with the mouth one confesses, resulting in salvation."

It's time for a dramatic change of approach. If we don't have bold faith, let's start asking boldly for the faith we lack. Imagine the love of a God who says, "It's true that without faith it is impossible to please Me. But I am so anxious to reward you with blessing, I'm even willing to supply the faith you lack. Ask Me, My child! Ask Me for what you lack! I am the only One who can help you overcome your unbelief!"

Though not seeing Him now, you believe in Him and rejoice with inexpressible and glorious joy.
    —1 Peter 1:8

*An argument started among them about who
would be the greatest of them.*
    —Luke 9:46

The latter part of Luke 9 contains several
seemingly disjointed snapshots of the
disciples. First, we see Jesus attempting to
penetrate their thick skulls with the
message of His soon-coming suffering
and death. But the Twelve didn't understand, and they were afraid to ask Jesus
what He meant. Instead, an argument
broke out among them about which of
them would be the greatest.

Can you imagine? Of course we can.

We are not much unlike Christ's original
disciples. They thought their argument
had been a private matter, but Christ

knew their thoughts, just as He does ours. We may never have argued with someone openly about our own great- ness, but Christ knows our hearts, as well as the attitudes that inhabit them.

He knows that our society thrives on ambition. And He knows that if we're not extremely discerning, we will bring these same ambitions into the church. He knows our biggest hindrance to greatness as Christians is our desire to be great.

Humble yourselves therefore under the mighty hand of God, so that He may exalt you in due time.
—1 Peter 5:6

When the disciples James and John saw this,
they said, "Lord, do You want us to call down
fire from heaven to consume them?"
    —Luke 9:54

Nothing is more permanent or terrifying
than the destruction of the lost. We ought
to be scared to death to wish such a thing
on anyone. Eternity is a long time. So
even when punishment comes to the
terribly wicked, we are wise to remember
with deep sobriety, humility, and
thankfulness that only grace saves us
from a like sentence.

Only one thing stands between us and
the lost: a blood-stained cross.

We know this world is filled with
wickedness. As Christ's present-day

disciples, we will no doubt be offended
when people reject the Savior the way the
Samaritan village did on this day. God's
desire, however, is for us to pray for His
mercy, for His Holy Spirit's conviction,
and for their repentance rather than their
judgment. Christ said even of those who
hammered the nails into His flesh,
"Father, forgive them, because they
do not know what they are doing"
(Luke 23:34).

Oh, God, give us a longing—not for the
sin of this world to be judged—but for
the sinners of this world to be forgiven.

*Your speech should always be gracious,
seasoned with salt, so that you may know how
you should answer each person.*
    —Colossians 4:6

Whoever rejects you rejects Me. And whoever
rejects Me rejects the One who sent Me.
   —Luke 10:16

In many ways, Jesus says to those who
belong to Him and who seek to do His
will: "Don't take rejection personally. Let
Me take it for you." Only Christ can take
rejection without being personally
incapacitated or hindered by it.

Who can begin to estimate the mileage
Satan gets from rejection? We have an
overwhelming tendency to take it
personally. From a bit of rejection, Satan
can get anything from a mile of discour-
agement to a thousand miles of despair.
But Christ says to us, "Let Me take it
personally for you. It can hurt Me,
but it can't hinder Me."

That's because only Christ can properly respond to rejection, while we are often powerless to do anything about it. In fact, our attempts at responding to it often make the situation worse. We don't fully understand what lies at the heart of rejection. We cannot judge another person's intention or motive.

But we can always trust Christ's big shoulders, Beloved, to be strong enough to take whatever others dish out.

Therefore, the person who rejects this does not reject man, but God, who also gives you His Holy Spirit.
   —*1 Thessalonians 4:8*

*In that same hour He rejoiced in the Holy
Spirit and said, "I praise You, Father, Lord of
heaven and earth."*

    —Luke 10:21

The word for Jesus' joy means "to exult,
leap for joy, to show one's joy by leaping
and skipping, denoting excessive or
ecstatic joy and delight." In the Septua-
gint of the Psalms, this idea often spoke
of "rejoicing with song and dance."

Someone may ask, "Do you expect me to
believe Christ jumped up and down with
ecstatic joy?" I don't have one bit of
trouble believing it! "Could the word
simply mean He rejoiced in His heart?"
Possibly, but the essence of the word is
what happens when rejoicing gets
physical!

You may apply it either way, but I prefer
to jump up and down with Jesus. With all
my heart, I believe Christ Jesus was and
is demonstrative.

Oh, Beloved, give Him a chance to leap
and dance over you! Dare to do what He's
calling you to do! And don't always be so
reasonable. I have a feeling there's one
thing Christ likes better than leaping and
skipping and dancing over you. How
about *with* you? So when you hear that
victory music playing, get up out of that
chair and shake a leg.

*How happy is the one whose transgression is
forgiven, whose sin is covered!*
    —Psalm 32:1

An expert in the law stood up to test Him,
saying, "Teacher, what must I do to inherit
eternal life?"
   —Luke 10:25

Scripture describes Jesus' questioner as
an expert in the law. His job was to
interpret the law of Moses the way
modern lawyers interpret the Constitu-
tion. He considered himself such an
expert that he intended to make Jesus
look foolish. So Jesus responded to him
with a question that means little to us but
was very familiar to the lawyer. He asked,
"How do you read it?"

Being forced to "go first," the legal mind
delivered the correct answer according to
Old Testament law: "Love the Lord your
God with all your heart, with all your

soul, with all your strength, and with all your mind; and your neighbor as yourself." The conversation could have stopped when Jesus said, "Do this and you will live." Instead, the lawyer just had to ask one more question: "And who is my neighbor?"

Do you hear a change in tone? The man wanted to justify himself—to show himself righteous—but why? Who said he wasn't? Christ didn't say a single condemning word to him. Jesus simply told him his answer was correct and to go live his answer.

When pride comes, disgrace follows, but with humility comes wisdom.
    —Proverbs 11:2

*Martha was distracted by her many tasks, and
she came up and asked, "Lord, don't You care
that my sister has left me to serve alone?"*
—Luke 10:40

I have a feeling if someone had asked
Martha's sister Mary at the end of the day
if Christ cared about her, she would have
answered affirmatively without hesita-
tion. But Martha came to Christ and
asked, "Don't You care?"

Christ's love for us never changes, but
our *sense* of His loving care can change
dramatically over time. And I believe the
determining factor in whether we sense
His love or not is our willingness to abide
in Him, to seek to practice a relationship
in which we develop a keener awareness
of His presence.

Sometimes we are so shocked when a seasoned servant of God confesses that he or she is struggling with belief and awareness of God's loving care. We might think, "You of all people! You're such a wonderful servant of God. How can you doubt for a moment how much He cares for you?" Could it be that somehow service has distracted them from abundant, life-giving intimacy?

Don't neglect to give Him ample opportunities to lavish you with the love He always feels for you.

She had a sister named Mary, who also sat at the Lord's feet and was listening to what He said.
    —Luke 10:39

When one stronger than he attacks and overpowers him, he takes from him all his weapons he trusted in, and divides up his plunder.

—Luke 11:22

Our "someone stronger" is going to take away Satan's armor and divide up the spoils. Do you know what this means to us? Jesus Christ is going to steal back what Satan has stolen from us! And guess what—not all the spoils have to wait until we're in heaven!

I can readily cite a personal example. Even though Satan stole many things from me through my childhood victimization, I am finally ready to say that God has given me back more than my enemy took. The enemy has fought against me with his weapons of shame, secrecy, and deception, but the plunder my Lord has won back for me has finally tipped the scale.

Through the many response letters I've received from my writings on the subject, I believe I can now say that the grace gift of seeing others helped through the power of the Holy Spirit has begun to outweigh the many years of pain that resulted from the abuse. The strong man may have put up a good fight, but his fight was no match for my stronger Man's muscle.

Then all flesh will know that I, the Lord, am your Savior, and your Redeemer, the Mighty One of Jacob.
—Isaiah 49:26

When an unclean spirit comes out of a man,
it roams through waterless places looking for
rest, and not finding rest, it then says, "I'll go
back to my house where I came from."
—Luke 11:24

We were created by God to be inhabited
by His Spirit. We were not created to be
empty. The vacuum in every human life
does not yearn to be fixed. It yearns to be
filled. God can deliver us from a terribly
oppressive stronghold, but if we don't fill
the void with Him, we are terribly
susceptible to a relapse.

And I'm telling you, a second round of
the same demonic stronghold can be
more powerful than the first. Once we've
been delivered from a stronghold, if we
make ourselves vulnerable to it again, our

second encounter may be far worse. This is because Satan hates to lose. If he was defeated once, given the opportunity, he'll try harder the next time. Satan also knows that the empty space—if left uninhabited by Christ—leaves the victim with a voracious appetite.

So let's be sure we engrave this in our cranium: victory is not determined as much by what we've been delivered *from* as by what we've been delivered *to*. It's not enough to be swept clean and put in order. We must be filled full of God.

Know the Messiah's love that surpasses knowledge, so you may be filled with all the fullness of God.
    —Ephesians 3:19

*He then told them, "Watch out and be on
guard against all greed because one's life is not
in the abundance of his possessions."*
—Luke 12:15

Believing our great value to God frees us
from the need for riches because, as Jesus
said, "One's life is not in the abundance of
his possessions." Aren't you thankful to
hear that?

But I'm reminded of a friend's statement:
"We act out what we believe, not what we
know." If we believe our value to God and
believe our life does not consist in the
abundance of our possessions, why then
do we *have* such an abundance of
possessions? Perhaps we know Luke
12:15 with our heads, but we really don't
believe it with our hearts.

James 1:17 tells us our Father is the giver of all good gifts. Throughout all of eternity, we will be lavished in the limitless wealth of the CEO of the universe. Until then, we show ourselves to be sons and daughters of the one true God when we give, give, give. So let's keep shoving that abundance out the door to help others in need, and God will lay up treasures for us in His own divine storage lot.

The LORD your God has chosen you to be His own possession out of all the peoples on the face of the earth.
    —Deuteronomy 7:6

You also be ready, because the Son of Man is
coming at an hour that you do not expect.
    —Luke 12:40

Some things about God's ways make me
grin . . . like the way He knows our
tendency to play amateur prophet. He
puts all of us in our date-setting places by
basically saying, "The only thing I'll tell
you about My next visit is that you won't
be expecting Me." The urgency is to be
ready at all times. To keep our lamps
burning.

One of the shocks of the empty nest is
not having anyone to wait up for. Even
though waiting up is exhausting, it's a
reminder of close family relationships
and responsibility. So at this particular
season in my life, my heart is encouraged

to know that we still have Someone for whom to "leave the light on."

Christ's desire is that we live in such close involvement with Him that all we lack is seeing Him face-to-face. Oh, that God would create in each of us such an acute awareness and belief of His presence that we won't be caught off guard! That our faith will simply be made sight! That we'll be gloriously shocked but unashamed!

Dear friends, don't let this one thing escape you: with the Lord one day is like 1,000 years, and 1,000 years like one day.
    —2 Peter 3:8

*If that slave says in his heart, "My master is
delaying his coming," and starts to beat the
male and female slaves . . . that slave's master
will come on a day he does not expect him.*
—Luke 12:45–46

I'd like to suggest that Jesus' picture of
the head servant beating the menservants
and maidservants while the master was
away could easily represent spiritual
abuse at the hands of religious leaders.
There are many forms of such abuse—
some more heinous than others. But one
subtle form involves using Scripture or
the name of God to manipulate others.

I have very little doubt we will be called
to account for the times we have used
God's name to get what we want. A huge
penalty awaits those who possess a

knowledge of God yet persist in meanness and self-indulgence.

If not for the many authentic examples
of godliness, I would despair over all the
abuse I've seen in the religious community. But I know the future punishment
of the unfaithful will be fair: "Much will
be required of everyone who has been
given much." (Luke 12:48). That's fair.
But that's serious.

Here is our joy and security in the midst
of much being required: Christ is never
the author of spiritual abuse.

Put on the Lord Jesus Christ, and make no
plans to satisfy the fleshly desires.
    —Romans 13:14

He said to them, "Go tell that fox, 'Look! I'm driving out demons and performing healings today and tomorrow, and on the third day I will complete My work.'"
—Luke 13:32

When Jesus spoke of the miracle activity He would be doing "today and tomorrow," followed by "the third day," He spoke not in the immediate sense but in a future tense. In essence, Christ said, "I have a goal. I have work to do today toward that goal. I have work to do tomorrow toward that goal. But very soon that goal will be accomplished."

Perhaps Christ's use of the words "today," "tomorrow," and "the third day" suggest three segments of time in *our* lives, as well. Today is our now. The third day could represent the ultimate fulfillment of God's goals for our lives. And tomorrow could represent every moment between now and then. He will complete His work in us, too.

Nothing could turn Christ from His goal when He was here. Neither Herod nor any other power posed a threat to the plan. And when we live our lives according to God's will, no Herod in the world can thwart our efforts at reaching God's goal either. Not a Herod of sickness nor a Herod of crisis. Not even a Herod that seems to hand us over to death.

The Lord is faithful; He will strengthen and guard you from the evil one.
   —2 Thessalonians 3:3

Jerusalem, Jerusalem! . . . How often I
wanted to gather your children together, as
a hen gathers her chicks under her wings,
but you were not willing!
    —Luke 13:34

We see the heart of God on display as His
Son cries out for the citizens of Jerusalem
to come under His sheltering wings of
protection.

The Old Testament paints a similar
portrait in Psalm 91. These words fall
around us like a down comforter from
heaven. The psalmist wrote: "The one
who lives under the protection of the
Most High dwells in the shadow of the
Almighty" (Ps. 91:1). The implication of
this verse is that a place of safety—a
certain level of immunity from evil

onslaughts—exists for those who choose to dwell there.

Obedience to our Father's commands is the key to immunity from the enemy. Obedience is what positions us in the shadow of the Almighty. When we are living in obedience, any evil that comes against us will have to go through God first. This explains why Christ longed to gather the children of Israel into His arms the way a hen gathers her chicks under her wings . . . yet didn't. Why? Because they weren't willing. They chose their own will over Christ's, forfeiting the shelter of His wings.

Guard me as the apple of Your eye; hide me in the shadow of Your wings.
    —Psalm 17:8

While the son was still a long way off, his father
saw him and was filled with compassion.
—Luke 15:20

I wonder if the prodigal son in Jesus'
parable was pacing. And pacing. And
pacing. He could see his home in the
distance, but perhaps he couldn't bring
himself to walk that last mile. He looked
at his father's vast estate and glanced
down at his own poor estate. His clothes
were worn and filthy. Dirt under every
nail. His hair long and matted or shorn to
the skin to defend against lice. All at
once, he became aware of his own foul
smell. He was destitute. Degraded.

But the prodigal's father was looking for
his son in the distance.

Oh, friend, can you glimpse the heart of God? Do you realize that when you run from Him, He yearns for you every minute and cannot be distracted from His thoughts of you?

When God sees our poor estate and the ravaging effects of our foolish decisions, He doesn't just sit back and say, "She got what she deserved." He is filled with compassion and longs to bring us back home. Yes, we face consequences, but those consequences are a loving summons back to the Father.

When you were dead in trespasses and in the uncircumcision of your flesh, He made you alive with Him and forgave us all our trespasses.
    —Colossians 2:13

Woe to the world because of offenses. For offenses must come, but woe to that man by whom the offense comes.
   —Matthew 18:7

Christ didn't mean that in some cases people have no choice but to sin. He didn't absolve the one who sins from the responsibility to repent. He did mean, however, that conditions can exist and things can happen that so greatly increase the tendency toward sin that a terrible woe is due the responsible party.

What are these "offenses"—these things that cause people to sin? The Greek word is *skandalon*. The idea of our English word "scandal" is present in the meaning. It is defined as "the trigger of a trap on which the bait is placed, and which, when touched by the animal, springs and causes it to close, causing entrapment. It always denotes an enticement to conduct which could ruin the person in question."

Yes, the truth remains that we did take the bait. If we are to live consistently outside a trap, we must recognize our own responsibility. This doesn't minimize, however, the sin of the trapper. Christ appears to be saying, in verse 6, "If you have entrapped a weaker, more vulnerable person in sin, you're going to wish you had drowned in the deepest sea rather than deal with Me."

When you sin like this against the brothers and wound their weak conscience, you are sinning against Christ.
    —1 Corinthians 8:12

Be on your guard. If your brother sins, rebuke him, and if he repents, forgive him.
　—Luke 17:3

Christ's specific prescriptive in Luke 17:3–4 is to fellow believers when we sin against one another. Someone might ask, "Does this mean I have to forgive only other Christians?" No, indeed. Luke 11:4 clearly tells us we are to forgive "everyone" who sins against us. The difference may not be in the forgiveness but in the rebuke.

I believe Christ suggests a different method of dealing with a brother or sister's sin. We are called to be different in the body of Christ. If we are functioning as a healthy body, ideally we should be able to bring issues that affect us to the table with one another to dialogue and, when appropriate, even to rebuke or receive a rebuke.

Needless to say, a tremendous burden of responsibility falls on the one giving the rebuke. A huge responsibility also falls on the recipient, obviously, to rightly accept the rebuke. But if we would learn the art of giving and receiving an appropriate rebuke in the early stages of wrongdoing, we would guard ourselves more effectively against offenses.

Do not take revenge or bear a grudge against members of your community, but love your neighbor as yourself.
—Leviticus 19:18

Jesus said, "Were not 10 cleansed? Where are the nine? Didn't any return to give glory to God except this foreigner?"
   —Luke 17:17–18

In this healing account from Christ's ministry, the ten lepers' differences were eclipsed by their common condition. They were surely a mix of Samaritans and Jews. Christ never would have said that only a "foreigner" returned with thanks if none of the ten had been Jews. Yet the tragic plight of the lepers gave them far more in common with each other than their differences as Jews and Gentiles.

Aren't we the same way? Before we are redeemed, not one of us is better than the other. We are all in the same sad state— lepers outside the city gate. Lost and isolated. Marred and unclean—whether we've lied or cheated, devalued another human being, or committed adultery. Lost is lost.

But furthermore, found is found. All of us in Christ have received the free gift of salvation in one way only: the grace of God. When we judge a brother's or sister's sin as so much worse than our own, we are like lepers counting spots.

As the body is one and has many parts, and all the parts of that body, though many, are one body—so also is Christ.
   —1 Corinthians 12:12

"I have kept all these from my youth," he said.
 —Luke 18:21

Consider the abbreviated list of commandments Christ mentioned to the rich
young ruler—each of which concerned
man's relationship with man—and each
of which the ruler claimed to have kept
since boyhood: "Do not commit adultery;
do not murder; do not steal; do not bear
false witness; honor your father and
mother."

He would likely get some check marks
for keeping some or all of these—at
least in name only—that is, if he knew
nothing about lust being the same thing
as committing adultery in his heart, or
about that little "anger" issue that Christ
said was the same as murder.

How would you fare? Shall we call you perfection personified? Or is your halo slipping a bit?

As for me, am I thankful for a Savior! The rich young ruler needed one too. His good track record had certainly fogged up his mirror. Don't get me wrong. I like him. I'm even impressed with him, but I'd rather be saved than be like him!

For by grace you are saved through faith, and this is not from yourselves; it is God's gift—not from works, so that no one can boast.
   —Ephesians 2:8–9

*When Jesus heard this, He told him, "You still
lack one thing: sell all that you have and
distribute it to the poor, and you will have
treasure in heaven. Then come, follow Me."*
—Luke 18:22

One of the primary purposes of this
divine pinprick was to show the man he
wasn't perfect, nor would he ever be. I
really believe a second purpose may have
been to offer an authentic invitation for
the searching young man to follow Him.

I also believe Christ had a purely
benevolent purpose for this seemingly
harsh demand. Jesus looked at this young
man and saw a prisoner. The man wasn't
really the ruler; his possessions were.
Jesus pointed him toward the only path
to freedom. Sometimes when our

possessions have us, we have to get rid of them to be free.

Of course, Christ knew in advance what the young man would choose. When it comes right down to it, we all follow our "god." The ironic part about this story, however, is that the rich young ruler was grief stricken over his own choice. But unless his heart changed somewhere along the way, he lived the rest of his life with all that wealth and an empty heart. Perfection or a perfect substitute. He had neither, because he lacked Jesus.

Instruct them to do good, to be rich in good works, to be generous, willing to share, storing up for themselves a good foundation for the age to come.
—1 Timothy 6:18–19

When Jesus came to the place, He looked up
and said to him, "Zacchaeus, hurry and come
down, because today I must stay at your
house."

—Luke 19:5

I can almost picture Christ working His
way through the crowd as if totally
oblivious to the short man in a tall tree.
He suddenly looked up with complete
familiarity. "Zacchaeus," He said.

How in the world did Jesus know his
name? Maybe the same way He knew
Nathaniel's a few years earlier. But why
did Jesus say, "Today I must stay at your
house"? Why "must" He? Perhaps because
the Son lived to do the will of His Father,
and His Father simply could not resist a
display of interest in His Son.

The Father and Son have an unparalleled mutual admiration society. That day Zacchaeus may have had a pair of skinned knees and elbows that endeared a special dose of the Father's affections.

Luke 19:6 says Zacchaeus "quickly came down and welcomed Him joyfully." At once. I'm not sure God honors anything more in a man than a timely response to His Son. No doubt the chief tax collector had many regrets in life, but among them wasn't the time he wasted between Christ's invitation and his welcome.

May You hear in heaven, Your dwelling place, their prayer and petition and uphold their cause.
    —*1 Kings 8:49*

Jesus said, "How hard it is for those who have wealth to enter the kingdom of God!"
    —Luke 18:24

A rich young ruler. A chief publican named Zacchaeus. Both wealthy men. One walked away lost, while salvation lodged at the other's home. Both had the Son of God standing right there in front of them . . . willing and able to deliver. The difference was that one saw how much he had to lose. The other saw how much he had to gain.

Notice, Christ did not ask Zacchaeus to sell everything he had and give to the poor, as He did to the younger man. Maybe because once Zacchaeus regarded Christ as life's true treasure, his wealth didn't mean nearly as much to him.

A cynic might say, "Why did he only give away *half* to the poor?" Maybe because it took the other half to pay back all the folks he had cheated! Anyway, God isn't looking to take away our possessions. He is looking to make His Son our greatest possession.

If you're facing a choice right now between pressing forward and drawing back, look at these two men. Which one do you want to be more like?

We are not those who draw back and are destroyed, but those who have faith and obtain life.
    —Hebrews 10:39

When these things begin to take place, stand up and lift up your heads, because your redemption is near!
—Luke 21:28

I love eschatology—a fancy word for end-time events. Few subjects are more exciting to study than the glorious future awaiting us. Just don't lose your head over it! Bible topics are not meant to become our focus—not even critical themes like holiness and service. *Jesus* is our focus.

Among the many facts we know about Christ's return, the one that is most clear is this one: it will be unmistakable. Luke 21:27 tells us that people "will see the Son of Man coming in a cloud with power and great glory." Revelation 1:7 also makes it clear that Christ's return to this earth will be impossible to miss: "Look! He is coming with the clouds, and every eye will see Him, including those who pierced Him. And all the families of the earth will mourn over Him. This is certain. Amen."

So whether or not we can answer all the questions that come to our mind, you and I can be sure we are living in an era on the kingdom calendar that will climax with the visible return of Jesus Christ. It's unmistakable.

Look! I am coming quickly, and My reward is with Me to repay each person according to what he has done.
   —Revelation 22:12

Because lawlessness will multiply, the love of many will grow cold.
—Matthew 24:12

One key word characterizing the hastening conclusion of this age is "increase." Jesus described end-time events like "birth pains" (see Matt. 24:8), meaning the evidences will increase in frequency and strength.

Luke 17:26–30 states that the time of Christ's return will be like that of Noah or Lot. The Old Testament lends some important insight into the condition of those societies. I believe the end of time will parallel the days of Noah and Lot in many ways, but among them will be a dramatic increase in perversity. Can anyone deny that we are living at a time

of dramatic escalation in sexual sin?
Based on multiple characteristics of the
last days, I am convinced they have
already begun.

So if we're going to be, like Noah—
righteous people surrounded by a sea
of unrighteousness—we have no other
recourse than to radically refuse to
cooperate, choosing instead to fight back
proactively. If we're going to be victorious
in a latter-day society, we must become
far more defensive—and offensive—
in our warfare.

*The Lord Himself will descend from heaven
with a shout, with the archangel's voice, and
with the trumpet of God.*
  —1 Thessalonians 4:16

*The chief priests, the scribes, and the leaders
of the people were looking for a way to
destroy Him.*
　—Luke 19:47

Jesus was teaching at the temple during
the day, then retreating at night to the
Mount of Olives, which overlooked
the temple. I wish we could all sit on that
hillside together and look at the Holy
City for a while. Picture it in your mind.

I once sat near this place where Jesus
retreated. I couldn't help wondering what
went through His mind during those
days. On that temple mount God had
provided the substitutionary offering for
Isaac, an "advance" showing of the gospel
of grace. Now Christ was camped on the
mountain parallel to the place of sacrifice

at the temple, resolving to fulfill the gospel that had been preached to Abraham.

And, oh, by the way—"The Passover was approaching" (Luke 22:1). A new year on Israel's sacred calendar had just begun, as had the most sacred and critical year in all of human history—"the year of the Lord's favor" (Luke 4:19). Can you imagine the anticipation in the unseen places? The kingdom of God and the kingdom of darkness were rising to a climactic point on the divine calendar.

He has reconciled you by His physical body through His death, to present you holy, faultless, and blameless before Him.
    —Colossians 1:22

Then Satan entered Judas, called Iscariot, who was numbered among the Twelve.
    —Luke 22:3

If you are new to the study of Scripture, the thought that Satan could enter a disciple might be terrifying. But keep in mind that Satan entered Judas as opposed to Peter, James, or John, even though at times each of them had certainly revealed weakness of character. Satan was able to enter Judas because he was available. Judas followed Christ for several years without ever giving his heart to Him. The authentic faith of the others protected them from demon possession, albeit not oppression, just as it protects us.

The evil one methodically seeks to work in your life and mine. I am stunned at his working knowledge of my fairly well-disguised vulnerabilities—even those I didn't know I had. He possesses a surprising amount of patience to weave seemingly harmless events into disasters, while his subject often never sees it coming.

What is our defense? The Word tells us not to be ignorant! Wising up to what the Word has to say about Christ's authority and the devil's schemes has empowered me to throw some holy kinks into Satan's unholy plans for my life.

Put on the full armor of God so that you can stand against the tactics of the Devil.
    —Ephesians 6:11

Jesus sent Peter and John, saying, "Go and
prepare the Passover meal for us."
    —Luke 22:8

While every part of the Passover meal
was highly symbolic, it had no meaning
at all without the lamb. Peter and John's
detailed preparation involving the lamb
would soon be fulfilled in Jesus Christ,
of course. They may not have grasped the
significance at the time, but eventually
they "got it."

Peter and John are the only two of the
Twelve who were recorded referring to
Jesus as the Lamb. Many years later, Peter
would write of Jesus that we were
redeemed "with the precious blood of
Christ, like that of a lamb without defect
or blemish" (1 Pet. 1:19). For John's part,

Revelation 5 contains perhaps the most majestic passage in Scripture about the Lamb of God.

Is it coincidence that only these two apostles wrote about Jesus as the Lamb? Not on your life. Christ's ultimate goal in any work He assigns to us is to reveal Himself, either through us or to us. The Holy Spirit used the tasks He assigned Peter and John that day to reveal to them the Lamb of God, to deeply engrave these images and remembrances in their minds.

The Lamb who was slaughtered is worthy to receive power and riches and wisdom and strength and honor and glory and blessing!
—*Revelation 5:12*

He also took the cup after supper and said,
"This cup is the new covenant established by
My blood; it is shed for you."
  —Luke 22:20

Christ never took anything more
seriously than the cup of redemption He
faced that last Passover supper. His body
would soon be broken so that the Bread
of life could be distributed to all who
would sit at His table. The wine of His
blood would be poured into new
wineskins for all who would partake.

It was time's perfect night—a night when
the last few stitches of a centuries-old
Passover thread would be woven onto the
canvas of earth in the shape of a cross.
Sit and reflect.

O perfect Lamb of Passover,
Let me not quickly run.
Recount to me the blessed plot,
Tell how the plan was spun
That I, a slave of Egypt's lusts,
A prisoner of dark dread,
Could be condemned unto a cross
And find You nailed instead.

We have been sanctified through the offering
of the body of Jesus Christ once and for all.
    —Hebrews 10:10

*Who is greater, the one at the table or the one
serving? Isn't it the one at the table? But I am
among you as the One who serves.*
  —Luke 22:27

Are you like me? Do you want to be
made like Christ—but more through
His victories than His sufferings?
Thankfully, we have a Savior who is
willing to steadfastly walk with us even
when we take three steps forward and
two steps back.

If we often find ourselves in contrast to
Jesus' perfect character, we're not so
unlike His original disciples. Their
inability at the Passover table to pinpoint
who was the worst among them led to a
dispute over who was the greatest. Had
not Christ already dealt with them over

this issue? Being declared "guilty as charged," however, only condemns us. Left alone, it does nothing to change us. Like the apostles, we are slow to learn.

Recognizing that the disciples' sandals do indeed fit us, let's allow Christ to kneel in front of us, slip them off, and wash our feet. Oh, how we need Him to minister humility to us. Without it, He will vastly limit how much He ministers through us.

If I, your Lord and Teacher, have washed your feet, you also ought to wash one another's feet.
—John 13:14

Simon, Simon, look out! Satan has asked to
sift you like wheat. But I have prayed for you
that your faith may not fail.
    —Luke 22:31–32

The method of sifting wheat is to put it
through a sieve and shake it until the
chaff and tares and little stones rise to the
surface. The purpose, of course, is so the
actual grain can be separated and ground
into meal.

Satan's goal in sifting us is to make us a
mockery by showing us to be all chaff
and no wheat. Christ, on the other hand,
permits us to be sifted to shake out the
real from the unreal, the trash from the
true. The wheat that proves usable is
authentic grain from which Christ can
make bread.

Satan turned Peter's field trip into a field
day, but—praise Christ's faithful name—
he still couldn't get everything about
Peter to come up chaff. So Satan's plan
backfired. He surfaced some serious
chaff, to be sure, but Christ let Peter have
a good look at it. Then Christ blew the
chaff away, took those remaining grains,
and demonstrated His baking skills.
His goal was to let Satan sift out all the
Simon-stuff so Christ could use what
was left.

*We have this treasure in clay jars, so that this
extraordinary power may be from God and
not from us.*
   —2 Corinthians 4:7

After singing psalms, they went out to the
Mount of Olives.
   —Matthew 26:30

Jesus singing! How I would love to hear
that sound. When Jesus sang, did the
angels of heaven hush to hear His voice?
Or did they cease their song and join in
His? Did He sing tenor? Bass? Did Christ
and His disciples sing in harmony, or did
they all sing the melody?

How fitting that on this very night,
Christ would give voice to songs penned
centuries earlier just for Him. Tradition-
ally, every Seder or Passover celebration
ended with the latter half of the Hallel,
Psalms 115–118. Very likely Christ and
His disciples sang from these psalms.
Imagine the Son of God singing these

words as the seconds ticked toward the cross.

Whatever Christ sang as the Passover meal concluded that night, the words had significance for Him that the others could never have comprehended. I wonder if His voice quivered with emotion? Or did He sing with exultation? Perhaps He did both.

One thing we know: Christ, above all others, knew that He was singing more than words. That night He sang the score of His destiny.

I will take the cup of salvation and worship the Lord. I will fulfill my vows to the Lord in the presence of all His people.
    —Psalm 116:13–14

*Abba, Father! All things are possible for You.
Take this cup away from Me. Nevertheless, not
what I will, but what You will.*
—Mark 14:36

Never minimize this moment by
thinking God couldn't have removed the
cup. Do not subtract God's freedom of
choice from this picture. God could have
chosen to reject the way of the cross.
After all, He is the sovereign of the
universe. That God could have stopped
the process—yet didn't—is a matchless
demonstration of love. Can you think of
anyone for whom you'd watch your only
child be tortured to death?

The request Christ placed before the
Father ought to make us catch our breath.
It ascended to heaven through wails of

grief. God's beloved was overwhelmed with sorrow to the point of death. Luke's Gospel tells us His sweat dropped like blood, a condition almost unheard of except when the physical body is placed in more stress and grief than it was fashioned to handle. Do we think God sat upon His throne unmoved?

Our hearts ought to miss a beat. Christ could have walked past the cross. He could have—but He didn't.

Because of Christ, I am pleased in weaknesses, in insults, in catastrophes, in persecutions, and in pressures. For when I am weak, then I am strong.
  —2 Corinthians 12:10

The Lord turned and looked at Peter. So Peter
remembered the word of the Lord, how He had
said to him, "Before the rooster crows today,
you will deny Me three times."
—Luke 22:61

Like Peter, I also made some choices in
my past that went beyond rationalization.
How thankful I am now that I couldn't
just make excuses for my behavior,
because any part of me I could have
"excused" would still be "alive and
kicking."

I want no part of myself. *None.* I want
Jesus to so thoroughly consume me that I
no longer exist. One regret I will never
have is that God got me "over myself" by
letting me confront this truth: in me
dwells no good thing.

I do not doubt that Christ's face was
painted with pain when His and Peter's
eyes met in the courtyard, but I think the
conspicuous absence of condemnation
tore through Peter's heart. I wonder if
Christ's fixed gaze might have said
something like this: "Remember, Peter, I
am the Christ. You know that, and I know
that. I called you. I gave you a new name.
I invited you to follow Me. Don't forget
who I am. Don't forget what you are
capable of doing. And whatever you do,
don't let this destroy you."

He is always able to save those who come to
God through Him, since He always lives to
intercede for them.
    —Hebrews 7:25

They all asked, "Are You, then, the Son of
God?" And He said to them, "You say that
I am."
   —Luke 22:70

Aren't you thankful humanity can "try"
Christ for being anything they choose,
and yet He remains who He is? No
amount of disbelief can change Him or
move Him. Why did the chief priests and
teachers of the law disbelieve? Why
couldn't they accept their Messiah?
Because they wanted to be king of the
mountain themselves.

And so our Savior was stripped. Mocked.
Spat upon. Struck . . . again and again.
Flogged. Beyond recognition. The
fullness of the Godhead bodily. The
bright and morning Star. The Alpha

and Omega. The anointed of the Lord.
The beloved Son of God. The radiance of
His Father's glory. The Light of the world.
The Hope of glory. The Lily of the valley.
The Prince of peace. The Seed of David.
The Son of righteousness. The blessed
and only Potentate, the King of kings,
and Lord of lords. Emmanuel. The With
of God.

The most terrifying truth a mocking
humanity will ever confront is that no
matter how Jesus is belittled, He cannot
be made little. He alone is King of the
mountain.

*Go and serve your idols, each of you. But
afterwards you will surely listen to Me, and
you will no longer defile My holy name.*
    —Ezekiel 20:39

Pilate, wanting to release Jesus, addressed them again, but they kept shouting, "Crucify! Crucify Him!"
—Luke 23:20–21

Nothing was accidental about the cross of Christ. The Son of God was not suddenly overcome by the wickedness of man and nailed to a cross. Quite the contrary, the cross was the means by which the Son of God overcame the wickedness of man.

The cross is the open door no man can shut. To secure the keys to the house of David and open the door of salvation to all who would enter, God drove His Son like a nail in a sure place.

A firm place. An enduring place.

I will never fully grasp how such human atrocities occurred at the free will of humanity, while God used them to unfold His perfect, divine, and redemptive plan. Christ was nailed to the cross as the one perfect human. He was the fulfillment of the law in every way. When God drove His Son like a nail in a firm place, He took the written code, finally fulfilled in His Son, and canceled our debt to it. With every pound of the hammer, God was nailing down redemption.

I will drive him, like a peg, into a firm place. He will be a throne of honor for his father's house.
 —Isaiah 22:23

*Jesus said, "Father, forgive them, because they
do not know what they are doing."*
   —Luke 23:34

Not "Father, consume them," but "Father,
forgive them." This may be the most
perfect statement spoken at the most
perfect time since God gave the gift of
language. As unimaginable as His request
was, it was so fitting! If the cross is about
anything at all, it is about forgiveness.
Forgiveness of the most incorrigible and
least deserving.

I don't believe the timing of this statement was meaningless. It was the first
thing He said after they nailed Him to
the cross and hoisted it into view. His
immediate request for the Father's
forgiveness sanctified the cross for its

enduring work through all of time. His request baptized the crude wood for its divine purpose.

Surely in the days to come, many involved were haunted by their consciences. No doubt many in the crowd at the Crucifixion were saved on the Day of Pentecost, since both events occurred in Jerusalem only weeks apart and on major feast days. The main reason to believe that these were the same people is because God doesn't ordinarily refuse the request of His Son.

Just as the Lord has forgiven you, so also you must forgive.
    —Colossians 3:13

Jesus cried out with a loud voice, "Elí, Elí, lemá
sabachtháni?" that is, "My God, My God, why
have You forsaken Me?"
   —*Matthew 27:46*

The curtain drops on our scene in the
form of darkness, which lasted three
hours. The Light of the world was about
to be extinguished, if only for a brief
time. Just before He breathed His last,
Jesus cried out with a loud voice, "Father,
into Your hands I entrust My spirit"
(Luke 23:46). How appropriate that He
would use His last breaths to utter the
trust upon which His entire life had
rested.

But I'm not sure we can properly
appreciate these words of faith unless we
consider the ones spoken by Him only

moments before. I believe this cry, "My God, my God, why have You forsaken Me?" marked the exact moment when the sins of all humanity—past, present, and future—were heaped upon Christ. Somehow I believe that to bear the sin, Jesus also had to bear the separation. But I am moved that He breathed His last breath with full assurance of His Father's trustworthiness.

The human body of the life-giver hung lifeless. It was finished. He gave up His last human breath so He never had to give up on humanity.

The Lord is my helper; I will not be afraid. What can man do to me?
    —Hebrews 13:6

She saw two angels in white sitting there, one at the head and one at the feet, where Jesus' body had been lying.
—John 20:12

The Old Testament tabernacle contained a marvelous picture foreshadowing this moment. The ark of the covenant represented the very presence of God. In Exodus 25:17–22, the very specific instructions for the mercy seat on the ark of the covenant demanded the cherubim to be in exactly this position—"one cherub at one end and one cherub at the other end . . . covering the mercy seat with their wings," facing each other.

Do you see the picture? No, I can't be dogmatic that the cherubim prefigured the angels at Christ's head and feet—

but I am personally convinced.

If the cherubim did prefigure the angels in the tomb, can you imagine how they guarded the body through the wait? With their wings overshadowing Him, they faced each other, looking toward the cover. Picture their reactions when the glorified body of Jesus sat up from the death shroud and walked out of the tomb, right through the rock. Wouldn't you have loved to hear as Christ thanked them for their service?

He demonstrated this power in the Messiah by raising Him from the dead.
  —Ephesians 1:20

Mary Magdalene, Joanna, Mary the mother of
James, and the other women with them were
telling the apostles these things.
  —Luke 24:10

Appointing these women as the first to
share the news of Jesus' resurrection was
a definite "custom shaker." Jesus knew the
apostles wouldn't believe them, but
perhaps He felt that the pending
discovery of their authenticity would
breed a fresh respect. After all, at the first
roll call in the post-ascension New
Testament church, you'll see women
listed as part of the first New Testament
cell group (see Acts 1:13–14).

For centuries the synagogue had kept
men and women separate. Now they
would be working and worshiping

shoulder-to-shoulder. Christ built His church on a foundation of mutual respect. Don't misunderstand. He wasn't prioritizing women over men. He simply took the ladder down to the basement where society had lowered women, and with His nail-scarred hands, He lifted them to a place of respect and credibility.

The last thing we women should want to do in the body of Christ is to take men's places. They have far too much responsibility for my taste! But by all means, let's do take our places! We have also been called to be credible witnesses of the Lord Jesus Christ.

There is no Jew or Greek, slave or free, male or female; for you are all one in Christ Jesus.
    —Galatians 3:28

Beginning with Moses and all the Prophets,
He interpreted for them the things concerning
Himself in all the Scriptures.
    —Luke 24:27

What I would give to have heard this comprehensive dissertation! Christ began with the books of Moses, went straight through the prophets, and explained what was said in all the Scriptures concerning Himself. One of the joys of heaven for me will be hearing a replay of this sermon!

The entire Old Testament was written about or toward Christ. Imagine Jesus Himself explaining the hundreds of ways the Scriptures predict and prepare for His coming. I could teach on this subject for hours, and I don't know even a fraction of

the ways Christ is taught in the Old
Testament.

Luke's use of "interpreted" in reference to
Christ's teaching means "to explain
clearly and exactly." I can't wait to know
"exactly" what some Scriptures mean.
Unlike me, Christ never had to say, "I
think . . ." or "I believe this means . . ."
He knew. What a Bible lesson these two
men heard! A lesson that would have
taken forty years of wilderness wander-
ings for me, Christ delivered with
glorious precision over a few Emmaus
miles. No wonder the two men hated to
part with Jesus!

*If you believed Moses, you would believe Me,
because he wrote about Me.*
　—John 5:46

He said to them, "Peace to you!" But they were
startled and terrified and thought they were
seeing a ghost.
—Luke 24:36–37

I have to laugh out loud from the
delightful irony that Christ's greeting of
peace nearly scared the disciples to death.

Just minutes earlier they were cheering,
"It is true!" But somehow when they
came face-to-face with Jesus, the sight
was almost more than they could bear.

I can almost hear Christ saying, "Boys,
you don't have a mental file already
prepared to stick this information in.
This one won't compute intellectually.
Quit trying. Just behold and believe."

I delight in knowing our future will be somewhat similar. You and I have banked our entire Christian lives on the fact that Jesus is very much alive, yet I have a feeling when we actually behold Him, it will only be eternal life that keeps us from dropping like dead men.

We have often seen His hands through constant provision and glorious intervention. We have often seen His feet as He's gone before us. Surely we have beheld the hands and feet of Christ with eyes of faith. Let us not be afraid, but only believe.

Now may the God of peace, who brought up from the dead our Lord Jesus . . . equip you with all that is good to do His will.
    —Hebrews 13:20–21

After worshiping Him, they returned to
Jerusalem with great joy.
    —Luke 24:52

Not one of these disciples was sorry He
had come their way. Their losses were
incalculable. Yet they left the Mount of
Olives with great joy, continually praising
God, for their ordinary lives had been
interrupted by glory. The sufferings of
this world simply could not compare to
the glory He had revealed to them. It
sustained and swelled them long after the
visible became invisible.

And you and I are the spiritual descen-
dants of those who offered their lives, not
for what they thought or what they
hoped, but for what they knew. For
whom they knew.

Jesus the One and Only—this title is His forever. He was the One and Only long before He breathed a soul into humanity, and He will continue to be the One and Only long after the last soul has been judged.

He is changeless. But you and I were destined for change. We cannot draw near Him and remain the same. May our tenure on this planet be characterized by one simple word . . .

Jesus!

Indeed, we have all received grace after grace from His fullness.
    —John 1:16

There is a Name above all names
Let mine be lost in His
Hide me in His crimson heart
O, way of secret bliss!

One life alone is worth the find
Nail mine onto the tree
Till Jesus ever shining here
Is all beheld in me.

Bring Him forth each day I live

And leave me in the tomb

I seek no other glory here

Make not the smallest room

Blessed anonymity!

Count my life but loss.

Jesus the One and Only

Tread over me, Dear Cross.